HOW IS A CRAYON MADE?

Written and Photographed by
OZ CHARLES

Simon and Schuster Books for Young Readers
Published by Simon & Schuster, New York

The author wishes to thank Binney & Smith Inc., the producers of Crayola crayons, for granting me complete access to their facilities and for their patience and generous cooperation in allowing me to photograph their unique manufacturing process.

The author wishes to thank Sinar Bron, Inc. for the use of their photographic studio.

With special thanks to Pamela D. Pollack, Grace D. Clarke, and Sylvia Frezzolini.

Designed by Sylvia Frezzolini
Manufactured in the United States of America

10   9   8   7   6   5   4   3   2   1

Library of Congress Cataloging-in-Publication Data
Charles, Oz.   How is a crayon made?
Summary: Describes, in text and step-by-step photographs, the manufacture of a crayon from wax to finished product.   1. Crayons—Juvenile literature.   [1. Crayons]   I. Title.   TS1268.C46
1988   741.2′3   87-11463
ISBN 0-671-63756-8

For Ian and Dillon

It's hard to imagine a world without crayons. If all the regular size crayons made in the United States last year were laid end-to-end around the equator, they would circle the globe four and a half times! Most people have crayons; but how are they made?

The first step in making a crayon is the creation of the color, which takes place at the color mill. Water and various chemicals are mixed in big wooden tanks to create the pigments that give crayons their color. Each pigment is made in a separate tank. The tanks are made of wood rather than metal, because metal would interfere with the chemical reaction that creates the colors.

Each color solution then passes through a filter press that squeezes out extra water, leaving moist cakes of color.

The cakes of color are scraped off the press, broken up by hand, and put into stacked plastic trays.

The plastic trays are put into a kiln to dry. They bake for three to four
days, leaving hard chunks of color.

The colored chunks are sent to blending machines, where they are
mixed according to special formulas to create different shades.

Next, a machine called a pulverizer, which is like a meat grinder, grinds the blended colors into a fine powder. The powder is put into bags, weighed, and sent to the crayon manufacturing plant.

Outside the plant are many storage tanks that hold heated liquid wax. Each tank is 26-feet high and holds 17,000 gallons of wax.

Liquid paraffin wax is pumped, through large pipes...

into mixing vats inside the plant.

Now, powdery colored pigment is poured into each vat of clear wax.

A rod inside the mixing vat stirs the colored pigment
and the clear wax, creating colored wax.

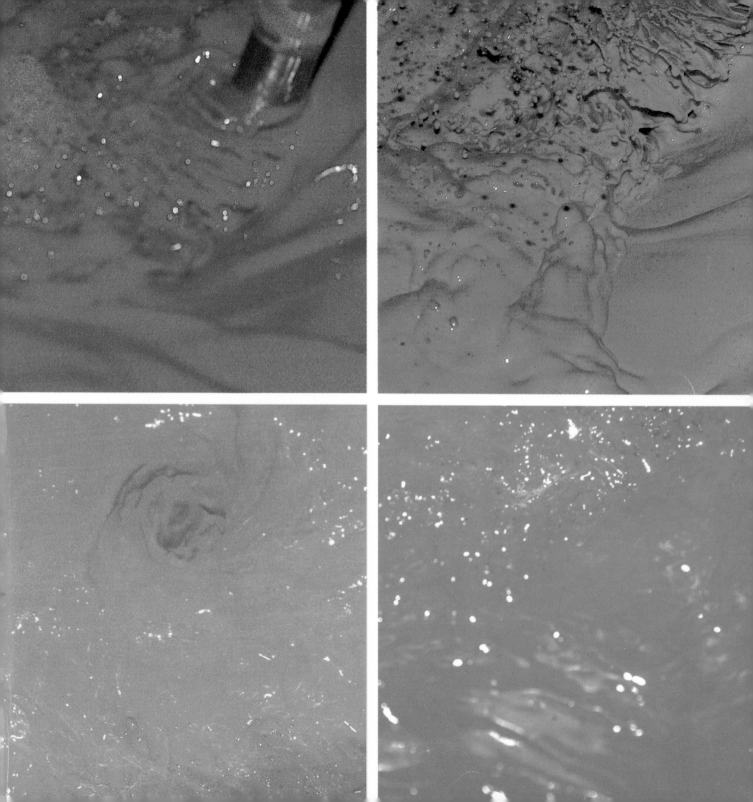

The colored wax, heated to about 240 degrees Fahrenheit, is piped from the mixing vat onto rotary mold tables. The rotary mold table is like a giant muffin tin with thousands of little holes. The wax flows into the holes, which are molds for the crayons. Each table has 2,426 molds.

While the wax is being poured, a spinning blade prevents bubbles from forming inside the crayons, and keeps the consistency smooth and free of lumps.

The rotary mold table moves slowly in a circular motion. Inside the table are pipes filled with cold water—between 40 and 70 degrees, depending upon the color crayon being made. The hot wax is cooled by the water for four to seven minutes—again, depending upon the color being made. As the wax cools, it hardens.

Excess hardened wax is scraped off the top of the table, to be remelted later for re-use.

The crayons left inside the molds are then ejected into a square metal frame with little holes, one for each crayon. Each hole contains a rod at the bottom.

The frame moves away from the table, and the rods push the crayons into an inspection bin. The crayons are checked for broken tips or chipped butt ends. Damaged ones are returned to the mixing vat to be melted and remolded.

The crayons are then fed, one by one, by conveyor belt into a labeling machine. Each rotary table has dual labeling machines for the color being made.

The labeling machines wrap and glue the label around each crayon. The labeled crayons are picked up by the operator running the machine and checked again for broken tips.

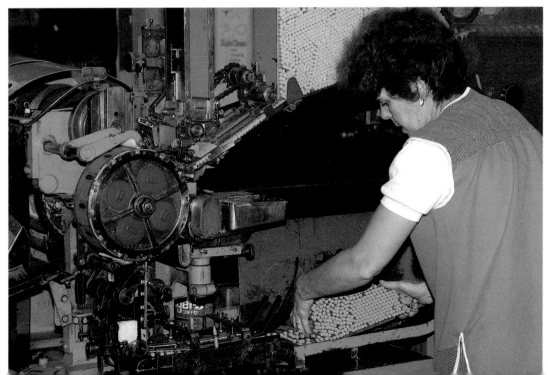

Meanwhile, a small number of crayons from each batch have been taken to the quality control lab to be tested.

A transverse breaking machine, or crayon eater, checks the crayons for strength. Electrically operated, the machine consists of a beam that acts like a fulcrum or pulley. It puts different amounts of pressure on the crayons at different points. If the crayon breaks sooner than it is supposed to, the batch from which it came is remelted and molded again.

Crayons are also tested for intensity of color. Is the red bright enough? Is it too pale, or too dark? They are even tested for consistency. Does the wax lay down smoothly on the paper? Is it lumpy? Is there a waxy build-up?

After the samples have passed the quality tests, the undamaged labeled crayons are scooped up and packed into wooden crates.

Crates of same-color crayons are moved by forklift to the packing area.

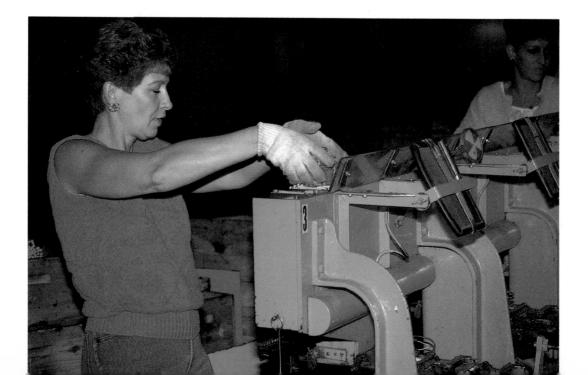

The crayons are put into packing machines that have different slots for different colors.

Just as a candy-vending machine sorts the different coins you put in and drops your selection, the packing machine sorts and arranges the crayons into different color assortments.

Narrow cardboard boxes, called sleeves, enter the machine flat.
The machine opens them, and puts in the color-assorted crayons.

Another packing machine, called a boxing machine, puts an assortment of crayon-filled sleeves into crayon boxes—like the ones you see in stores. Different machines can box anywhere from 6 to 64 crayons.

The finished boxes are then packed and shipped to the warehouse where they are loaded onto trucks and delivered to the stores. They are ready to be bought, taken home, and used—and the rest is up to you!